First Edition Reviews

Vivianne on Amazon Says:

"I initially got this book among others because of its price. I was very happily surprised by the contents of the book. The author explains why forgiveness is a gift to ourselves and something I did not know, that forgiveness is more efficient if we start forgiving ourselves first. She also gives several simple and effective techniques and tips on how to move on which for me was critical. I do not want to spoil it for you so I will not say more. But if you are looking for an excellent book for forgiveness, this is it. I plan to practice what she said for 30 days and I am sure something will change as I am already starting to feel that I am able to let go. This is a true miracle. What is interesting is that my letting go is not superficial, the book helped me get clear on why this was a gift to myself. A gift of peace. And this is where my resolve came from. This book helped me build the resolve from the heart, to let go. I highly recommend it. You will be pleased. This book is transformative. The consciousness with which the author wrote the book is truly transformative for the reader. Do not be fooled by the price. This is a high level quality book."

Letting Go:

HOW TO FORGIVE &
TRANSFORM YOUR LIFE

Judene Elizabeth

BALBOA.
PRESS

A DIVISION OF HAY HOUSE

Balboa Press books may be ordered through booksellers or by contacting:

Balboa Press
A Division of Hay House
1663 Liberty Drive
Bloomington, IN 47403
www.balboapress.com
1 (877) 407-4847

Because of the dynamic nature of the Internet, any web addresses or links contained in this book may have changed since publication and may no longer be valid. The views expressed in this work are solely those of the author and do not necessarily reflect the views of the publisher, and the publisher hereby disclaims any responsibility for them.

The author of this book does not dispense medical advice or prescribe the use of any technique as a form of treatment for physical, emotional, or medical problems without the advice of a physician, either directly or indirectly. The intent of the author is only to offer information of a general nature to help you in your quest for emotional and spiritual well-being. In the event you use any of the information in this book for yourself, which is your constitutional right, the author and the publisher assume no responsibility for your actions.

Any people depicted in stock imagery provided by Thinkstock are models, and such images are being used for illustrative purposes only. Certain stock imagery © Thinkstock.

Print information available on the last page.

ISBN: 978-1-5043-2573-8 (sc)
ISBN: 978-1-5043-2574-5 (e)

Library of Congress Control Number: 2014922815

Balboa Press rev. date: 03/18/2015

Contents

ACKNOWLEDGMENTS

I would like to gratefully acknowledge several people. My husband, Ernest. Without his endless patience and intense love, the Joie de vivre would not exist in my life. I am grateful this transformation gives me the opportunity to give back to our love.

My Mother and Father who were always there to believe in me, they've shown me the vast abilities of love and courage.

All the brave souls doing the work within which is necessary to transform our world. Great job!

The truth seekers I mention in Chapter Five, showing us facts we can trust, raising our awareness and proving we have the power to achieve our goals.

INTRODUCTION

In this book, I will show you how to forgive yourself and others. In addition, I provide useful insight and valuable tools to help you change negative habits into positive fuel. Having been through this personally, I know it works.

This system was created after many years of turmoil. After trying numerous different methods I have found this to be the most effective way to be free. Since I have done this, I have been told by family, friends and strangers alike that I am glowing, positively radiant. They can't tell what it is but they know something is different, special.

Now I'm happy, confident and organized. I am truly living the life I've always wanted. It is my greatest wish for you to be set free and start living the life you've always wanted. So let's get started.

Chapter One

FORGIVENESS HEALS!

Congratulations, for taking the time to learn how. You've taken the first step toward a more rewarding life. This book not only provides the exercises that will help you forgive and let go, it also covers insights into our thinking, a way to throw out the old and create new habits that align with our bliss. It is not for the faint of heart but it is for those who yearn for a better life.

Forgiveness isn't just an act, it's *the* act that saves us. As we will come to know, forgiveness is everything, connected with everything we do, think and are, even dictates who we can be. It is the most important act we can do to advance our growth and success. A lot of people don't understand how much hurt they carry around, not understanding why they are always depressed or feel fatigued. We can unlock these feelings and our prison doors. We can be set free with a little inside work.

It does take effort and obviously, it's very personal, the answer can not be handed out like a pill. It's more like an equation and the variable that makes it work is *You*. One has to want it, make a commitment to the necessary changes in the heart and mind.

This is in part why this material has been misconstrued as some sort of secret. Being conveyed as almost arcane in nature, it has been touted as the kind of information one could only receive in a religion or secret society. This is simply not true. This information is for everyone. This work will benefit all of mankind. Will you imagine if everyone holding a grudge or hated themselves suddenly turned to love and forgiveness—Wow!

If you've ever found it difficult to forgive people, you're not alone most people have similar issues, but maybe you've overlooked the fundamental key. It's a missing link, that really helped me. The little-known fact is: forgiveness starts within! Transformation comes from within each individual differently and not everyone is willing to do what is necessary.

Yes, forgiveness can be difficult. Believe me, I realize when someone has hurt you or abused your trust, you may think something has died inside of you that can't be brought back. But here's the point, we don't have to bring it back. We don't need to have things the way they were or reach out to that person. We don't have to call them and hope they're also ready. We just have to access that part, deep inside us, where they still dwell and hurt us.

When we have the guts to make that journey deep inside ourselves and root around, amazing, miraculous things start to happen. With self-reflection and courage we can reach that part where the hurt resides and clear the space. So we don't have to go outward, call anybody, or ever see them again, this isn't the 12 steps. This is one step—*within.*

There is an acceptance that needs to take place before we can truly start taking care of ourselves. The realization that we are all one. That is to say, there is a part of you in me and a part of me in you. If we've done someone wrong or been wronged, we only need to reach inside ourselves to that particular part which represents the person or hurt and clear the space.

With forgiveness we get our clarity back and we get our life back. When you reach inside you'll realize forgiving yourself means forgiving all others. It means starting fresh with the whole world. New feelings plus new in-look equals a new outlook. That's how we do it, we reach in and find that part of us where hurt still dwells and make room for something new. Then we change our patterns of thought to match our goals.

When we tear down the barriers and let the light in we are free. Instead of negative energy stealing our power, we can be empowered by the opportunity available to us. This is what people fail to realize. We lose a lot of creative possibility and energy when we harbor resentments, don't practice gratitude and refuse to forgive ourselves and others. Negative energy makes us sick and hopeless thoughts keep us sick. We need to understand this connection.

People consumed with a gloomy attitude are unable to see the beauty around them, they could miss a flower right in front of them. If it were pointed out, they'd say, "I didn't even notice that" because instead of seeing the beauty all they saw was the rain. Not seeing with flowered eyes but rainy eyes. These are the habits that need to be changed if we are to live a better life. We have a choice: Negative thoughts = Negative life; Positive thoughts = Positive life.

Negative thoughts steal our power, positive thoughts provide us with power. In fact, positive thoughts can serve as an internal power plant to our whole system. You don't have to believe me, try it and you'll see. It is said by many great teachers that approximately 30 days of a practice will create a habit. Well then, put it to the test. Do the forgiveness exercise in this book and attempt to mind your thoughts for at least 30 days and find out for yourself how miraculous this can be. What do you have to lose? Lots of old pain and UN-serving customs. I invite you to challenge yourself and see what happens.

Our body reflects what our mind provides. It's a connection talked about in every culture and language. Unfortunately, for those with constant inner turmoil, illness is the most common result of the mind/body connection phenomenon. I am now healed from the inside out and continue to heal everyday in every way. If we keep a healthy mind our body will follow, I don't even get ill anymore. I used to get a bad cold or flu twice a year, but since this practice I haven't been sick. When I start to feel strange, I simply reflect on my thoughts and make the necessary adjustments. Then I am tiptop again. The outside will always match the inside, it might take time, but eventually it will be noticed. Positive thoughts of gratitude and happiness, this is what we all want and it starts with forgiveness.

This is a time of great transformation, we can excel exponentially with a few minor changes. We cannot leave out forgiveness as a means of healing nor letting go as a way of returning to the rewarding life we are meant to live. Another way to think about life is to live in your possibilities. Most of us go around not only stressed out but without proper sleep, vitamins, food and over 90% of the population is dehydrated. We operate rather well, successfully in some cases, so my point is—imagine what we could accomplish if we took care of ourselves.

It must happen within. Let's start with the basics. In 'Wikipedia' forgiveness is described as "the renunciation or cessation of resentment or anger." This is the process of concluding a 'perceived event'. The Oxford English dictionary specifies forgiveness as "to grant free pardon and to give up all claim". These are two of the best descriptions I've seen. The first one uses the word cessation which is 'to stop or put an end to'. This is important to look at because a conclusion is best, we want to bring an end to our suffering. It is the very nature of the healing scale; we cannot move into healing until there is a conclusion of 'the event.'

The second explanation uses the phrase 'give up all claim' and this one is very important also because to give up all claim introduces a statement of non-judgment and releases you from your 'story'. Your story is your interpretation of what happened, usually involving a lot of drama. It doesn't have to be embellished with details because the healing comes when the details are given up. I want to repeat that, so you don't think it's a typo—the healing comes when the details are given up!

The exploration of the benefits of forgiveness is gaining popularity and even scientific perspective. As more studies and healing arts are shared with the public, I envision very exciting things to come. Certainly the phenomenon of healing has not gone unnoticed by the scientific community. Currently several brilliant minds are attempting to reshape our world and the way we perceive forgiveness and our thoughts.

In the past, the idea that forgiveness makes one feel better was left to religious beliefs and private, esoteric doctrines. Most religions include teachings on forgiveness but speak of it as a distant, elusive grand prize, difficult to attain and always given by someone else. We've lived with an idea that it cannot be achieved from within or it is not ours to give and we are saturated with the sentiment that we are unworthy.

We're instructed to look outward, upward, elsewhere and then wait and hope. I believe we must be much more responsible in obtaining, respecting and living in this great healing power and energetic light. Even Jesus Christ said "The kingdom of heaven is within."

Let's look at some of the reasons we hurt. Poor communication and unfulfilled expectations are the root causes of pain. Making someone else wrong seems easier than taking responsibility. Letting go gives one access to the tame mind and again, releases one from their story. Unfortunately, one of the side effects of the meek soul is it can be mistaken for weakness, this is a terrible misconception and should be ignored by those who practice forgiveness. For this concept comes from the unaware mind and as discouraging as it may be, it is by no means a reason not to try.

The first step is in consciousness, waking up to the awareness that processing needs to take place, in some cases, lots of processing. We need to acknowledge that resentment, hatred, anger and grudges not good for us and they no longer serve. You must already have some degree of this awareness or you would not have picked up this book.

After this acceptance comes the hard part, the challenge and discipline. A commitment must be made to yourself to work through these issues at all costs. No matter how it makes you feel in the interim, you must have faith that all your hard work will be worth it in the end. And believe me, it is. We are on the Path of miracles.

Chapter Two

LETTING GO

There is a spiritual tag-team of the heart. This team consists of forgiveness, compassion and gratitude. They empower each other exponentially and together become a gateway to a new reality. Forgive yourself and others. Think and act with compassion. Live with gratitude. Together these open the door to letting go and a new way to being.

To get the absolute most out of life we have to be true to ourselves. So, we can't discuss forgiveness without discussing compassion. Compassion is the greatest expression of love and the finest gift anyone can receive. Sometimes its hard to find sympathy, but it always helps to attempt to put yourself in the others position. I'm a firm believer in the "walk a mile in my shoes" plan. Until we have taken this walk, we really don't know what another is going through. No matter how much we feel justified, we really can't judge. When you show compassion you have succeeded in this walk and we all possess this strength.

Many people think that the task of forgiveness is too daunting to even think about. People look at the world as a whole and tend to lump everyone together. Saying "how can I forgive, when I was wronged so badly?" or "how can I forgive a society capable of such cruelty?" Aah, but this is a key. We don't have to forgive every member of society, again, we don't have to seek out and forgive those that have done us wrong. All we have to do is forgive ourselves.

The act of forgiving oneself is the act of forgiving the world. Have you ever heard 'we are within the universe and the universe is within us?' Well, this statement may be more true than you could imagine.

Lewis B. Smedes says "To forgive is to set a prisoner free and discover that prisoner was you."

One misconception about forgiveness is that it's all about taking full responsibility. Certainly taking some is important but it's also about 'letting go' and not taking all the responsibility. It's interesting that when we don't take enough, we're downplaying our abilities, but when we assume we are to take it all, we are exaggerating our part. The right balance makes for a happy life and well adjusted memories.

Some say they are too enraged to forgive and I understand wrath also, I am one of the original angry people. Ultimately however, this gets us nowhere, but sick. Not living up to our true potential does nothing to teach other people a lesson or set them straight. Isn't being happy most important?

Some forgiveness exercises don't work because people are in different stages of their path. One, who may be ready and willing, might be met with more animosity from one who isn't. This may foil enthusiasm and squash attempts at a better life. Unfortunately, a thwarted plan can make some never want to try again and this is the real loss. So it's best to stick to one thing at a time and do the work within, where the real power exists.

Try to remember, when you're feeling low, in love's service only broken hearts qualify so if you've earned your credentials you're in a much better situation not only to love again but to help someone else.

The practice of compassion takes just that, practice. Truly caring is a constant task, sending love out to everyone can be exhausting but it gets easier with practice and the knowing that we are all one. Helping others is helping yourself and vise-verse.

Frederick Buechner tells us "Compassion is the knowledge that there can never really be any peace and joy for me until there is peace and joy finally for you too." After all, why choose depression or sadness anyway? Why do we pursue a potentiality that is not in line with what we want out of life? When we harbor resentments and practice hatred, we end up getting exactly what we didn't want. In a bizarre twist of fate, we give power to that which holds us back.

Funny, how we can hate ourselves, but then wonder why no one else seems to like us either. We walk around playing the "I hate myself" music with the "why don't more people like me" melody in the background. Then we can't understand why there is so much evidence to support our thoughts. I want to reiterate that coming to terms with this might make you uncomfortable, even feel sick to your stomach, but don't give up, a new life awaits. Be willing to sit through your discomfort and let your feelings flow. No matter how painful a memory can be, it still is what it is and isn't what it isn't! Often, much of the pain comes from refusing to experience feelings; fighting rather than letting them flow. From fight to flow, that's what this work is about.

Memories belong in the past and that's where they should stay. So how do we do this? Processing, giving up all claim and concluding. We need to let go of the perception of fault, rehearsing details of judgments and finally the judgments themselves. Do you really believe by harboring resentment for 20 years you have done anything to teach anybody a lesson? Has anything ever been solved by 'never speaking' to someone again? "Holding a grudge is like picking up a hot rock from the fire, with the intent on throwing it at your enemy, you're the one getting burned."—Unknown

One of the biggest barriers to forgiveness is the limiting idea of 'who we are?' Who are we to forgive? This thinking needs to be illuminated, we need to remember who we are. We are an expression of Source, we are Source Light, Source Energy. When we remember this we will know our being. We must understand that forgiveness has to come from within, everything else is an illusion.

Resistance and fear are more hindrances to transformation and so is lack of intention. Looking at the study done in worldwide random number generators mentioned in chapter 5 shows undeniable proof that intention is a major key to any success. We must set forth a clear objective of what we want first; then once our thoughts are in place, our actions follow and our path is clear. This is a universal truth. If I ever want someone to like me, I must lead by example and like myself first. If I want to be forgiven, I must forgive myself and in doing so, set my soul free.

The actual truth is love is not elusive and forgiveness is not difficult, but we must get started. To concentrate on it won't work and it cannot be bought or swindled. One must realize blessings come to those who do the work. Real love has no expectations, but exceeds all dreams, has no boundaries, no limits, but never hurts or demands. I can't understand why someone wouldn't do anything to keep it, why a little isn't preferable to none at all, but each person is on their own path and love is also a lesson. Just as the tongue gets sharper with use, so the heart becomes stronger and more powerful with it's exercise.

The idea of love and forgiveness is passed down from generation to generation, but few have actually led by example to shine a light for our paths. Indeed, all those who have tried are very controversial figures in our world, but they are also great catalysts for change. When excuses are made as to why we can't forgive or achieve, opportunities are lost and we become victims of our own minds. Our bodies will eventually fall prey to this weakness and illness will appear, but this never has to be.

The people who say letting go is too difficult are the ones who either haven't tried or didn't try with a clear intention from the heart and they are very unhappy people. Letting go is necessary and carries with it great rewards. By developing a forgiving, compassionate and grateful spirit we open ourselves to receive the greatest gifts in life.

Chapter Three

How To Forgive

If there is work, this is it. However hard this may seem, I know by experience, it's worth it and this too shall pass. Understand that "Life either expands or contracts in direct proportion to your courage to forgive."—Unknown. Forgiveness is imperative for our evolution. If we cannot learn to give up the past we will never move beyond it, into the possibilities of now. Realize that your grudge and bitterness benefits you in no way. Many times people begin a grievance to satisfy an urge or to feel right. Right or wrong is not at issue here only how resentment destroys the body and mind. Living in the past overcomes the now and eliminates the possibility of good times that can be enjoyed today.

It becomes much easier to forgive people when you realize that hatred and unhappiness just gives you more details to worry about, scenarios to remember and takes up precious space in your thoughts. Realize that the best revenge is to rise above negative thinking and love your enemies. It was Oscar Wilde who said "always forgive your enemies, nothing annoys them as much." It's true, it frustrates unhappy people when they realize that their efforts to upset are in vain and what they do to break you just seems to make you stronger. You can say, "Thank you for that life lesson" and whistle on down the road. In this way we discover we have no enemies.

Our first instinct, of course, when offended is to retaliate. Any person might be expecting such a response, but we can rise above and be one step ahead by just resisting the urge to strike back. People will always offend us, but responding in kind only fuels the fire and causes more drama. The mind is not at rest when holding a grudge or when in a constant state of anger, living in the past and using all your energy for hatred makes one achy, tired, anxious and sad.

This is how people stay unhappy and get sick. Realize this and you're on the path of letting go. A wonderful start and good practice to get into is controlling your thoughts. Stop thinking negatively. This is usually the cause of most people's stress and their inability to forgive. Negative thoughts work hand-in-hand with negative emotions to create negative action. This must stop. If we are constantly thinking of the nonsupporting things people have done, we won't see them for the people they may have become since and we are never truly in the now. Four essential things I have come to know is, everyone makes mistakes, nobody's perfect, not everyone hates me and in the end being right isn't near as important as being happy.

Next, don't be a pessimists, it makes you miss out on the positives in life. Try to replace the negatives in your mind with positives. For each and every antagonistic thought you have, come up with an affirmative, in fact come up with two. Instead of remembering horrific details of a situation, make an effort to remember something, anything good, maybe you liked the paint on the wall. Try to come up with something positive, no matter how small.

Keep doing this with every thought that disturbs you, constantly finding something good to replace the negatives. At first, it may seem ridiculous but it uses your hard earned concentration on the *positive* practice of thought. Thinking positive trains your eyes and brain to see the silver lining.

This takes practice but is worth the time. Instead of repeating the same negative mantra, yelling how angry you are with a person, scramble your thoughts, remember that you live in the now and snap yourself back to it. Look up and around, notice your immediate surroundings, count your blessings and recite for what you are grateful. This gets easier with repetition. Be stingy about your now moments, don't trade them for experiences of yesterday. Even fun times of the past should not be revisited too often for it takes away from current opportunities to create even more joy in life.

By being grateful for every moment, it's unforced to live in the now and easy to give up the past. Breaking old thought patterns takes effort at first, constantly keeping your thoughts in-check. Over time new neural-pathways are created in your brain and the process starts to become effortless, even habitual. Your actions are the end result, your thoughts are what create your manifestations, tame them wisely.

Be willing to give up commitment to your position and make a commitment to be happy. This means to forfeit the need to be right. You don't do this to prove your better or make others wrong, you do it because *that what provides the clearing.*

Look at what you're really committed to shouldn't it be you and your happiness? First admit there's an opportunity for a better way, then own it. Give up position and open a conversation for new circumstances. Your life is your responsibility. You say how you feel. Remember, no one can make you feel worthless, only you can do that. Start to analyze every reaction and thought with the question, "What am I getting out of this"? If the answer is a negative or you're not sure don't go there.

Seek to climb out of your story. Ask yourself "what really happened there?" Then separate your story from the facts. Focusing on just the facts allows you to lose your story surrounding the incident and a lot of the emotional pain that goes with it.

The next step is to realize the details don't matter. It sounds like a paradox to say zero in on the facts and then forget them, but it's actually a very effective technique. Know and understand that the amount of drama doesn't matter either, again the healing begins when the story and details are given up. You're committed to your happiness now, nothing else matters. Decide to find a way to be empowered in everything. You'll find this will increase your energy, happiness and even your sense of humor. Over time your heart will delight in the smallest of things. Almost everything becomes funny as joy greatly empowers your new space.

Another effective processing technique is to attempt to be the 'fly on the wall' of your life. It's only natural to replay situations in your mind especially those that bring out strong emotions. However, replay it through your new perspective and gain new insights regarding the situation. If you are a fly on the wall during playback, instead of the victim, a separation is made and new eyes become available for healing realizations. Sounds silly, but it really works.

Another reason people are afraid to do this work is because of ridicule. Friends or family may ask why put yourself through it or say that those who endeavor in self-reflection are unusual. It's not unlike those who seek counseling being called crazy. But it's not crazy, ignore unenlightened opinions. This work is imperative. Bravo, to you doing the work necessary for better life! All of the things we think we are incapable of doing, like forgiving and showing compassion are haunting us and will continue until we deal with them. If getting through 2012 was about anything, it is a year for processing and change.

All things are coming to the surface and whatever we are not capable of accepting will be our undoing. If we cannot forgive, we will not be forgiven. If we cannot show compassion, we will not be shown compassion. These are some of the great truths of life. We must evolve. It takes more guts to look inside and open our heart than to shy away. I hear many say, "I could never do that, my can of worms is too big." or, "if I started crying I would never stop," and therein lies their prison. For these can no longer be excuses for not living a full life.

Now each time a negative thought provokes me to speak, I refuse! I will not give power to them by my speech. Controlling my thoughts, I don't always feel like I have to go back to the beginning every time I get upset. It's only one step back and I can regain that quickly by meticulously guiding my cognitive content. In this way, we begin generating the thought patterns that are effective in the face of breakdowns and stress.

Another little secret is the power of language. I've learned something very profound about language; that it is also in our language that prison cells be found. Our language is the source of most of our misconceptions. I will no longer support language that is not empowering and I will no longer reinforce language that hypnotizes me. Like reading the labels on food products, I now carefully select my speech.

There is a conditioned underlying language of society that says 'we do not have enough strength as individuals to actually do anything'. The farce is that we don't have power; we're told "there's nothing you can do". It's the common lie we tell ourselves about how things came to be. But it's just that—a lie. Every moment is a choice.

Every action and more importantly, we need to understand this, every _thought_ is a choice. These thoughts become our actions which become tomorrow's . . . 'How things came to be'! In other words, who we are, dictates what we do, which causes the experiences we have. So you see, we DO have power and it begins with our thoughts. I love what Mooji says about "Each thought should have to audition" - to get our energy and attention. Perfect!

In "As a Man Thinketh", an essay by James Allen, it is clear that our thoughts rule our world. "The soul attracts that which it secretly harbors, that which it loves, and also that which it fears." The title is influenced by a verse in the Bible from the book of Proverbs chapter 23 verse 7 "As a man thinketh in his heart, so is he." This is right on! I do not need to give in to negative thoughts or give power to self-doubt and futility. I only need to remember that just like an artist is creating a picture with every stroke of the brush, so too, am I creating my world with every thought. This has made such a difference in my life.

I'm so strong I actually get excited when I feel a breakdown coming for I know a breakthrough is right behind. I will learn something, practice strength and gain experience. By exercising and reveling in these new options, I feel positive energy coursing through my body and mind. My growth is so intense and exciting it continues to astound me everyday.

There are many hailed forgiveness exercises and I believe that ANY self reflection is great for the soul. I would like to share what I have learned to be most effective and what powerfully worked for me. In doing this exercise I have set my soul free. When I first went through this I just had no idea it would be this powerful or keep growing. It all started with forgiveness.

The exercise follows shortly, but first, I had a breakdown. I know I'm not the only one with self-loathing tendencies. There's always a huge list of items anyone can find that qualifies to lead one to a breakdown. Personally, I've always felt pummeled by life. In my despair, doubts and negative thoughts were all I could experience. I questioned everything. Most people have been here at some point in their life. Everything seemed to be on the line. I felt I was going crazy but strangely, it was an old familiar feeling. It's interesting what the human being can get used to, even when we are miserable we will still take familiarity over the idea of traveling to new territory or making an effort to change.

My anxiety was screaming "you can't do this and might as well not try", I bought into it for a little while and let my mind work overtime feeling depressed and powerless. I hurt myself every chance I could, overeating, heavy drinking, constantly beating myself up. Reliving my story in great detail. What was wrong with me? Why couldn't I move on? I couldn't get off the concept that "I'm not good enough". The "he said, she said" judgments, the feelings of fear, guilt, shame, sadness and loss can get overwhelming.

I knew I had to find a better way. I didn't want to go on suffering in that mode of living anymore. Finally, I decided it's time to make a real, lasting change. In the past I'd felt I was a very compassionate person. My thinking was that I was forgiving as I went along, giving an acceptable effort to being a good person. What I didn't realize at the time but have come to understand is that it starts within.

I thought by forgiving others I would be happy and I didn't understand why this way of thinking is a trap. One cannot claim love and forgiveness for other people, all the while deeply hating oneself. That's why I would be surprised every time things went wrong and I found myself quickly back to unhappy and unfulfilled.

I'd heard of many studies in quantum physics, psychology and other inspirational material discussing our world being a mirror of ourselves. So how could I have thought that I had truly forgiven anyone while never forgiving myself? Until we love ourselves, we cannot enjoy love from another or properly give love. However, once we let go and clear the energy that obstructs our path we are free to live a healthier and happier life. Free to love and receive love at will. Remember, the caterpillar must die for the butterfly to live.

Here is the exercise: Sit comfortably and take three deep breaths. When you inhale think of new beginning's. It may help to picture a healing color such as pink or light blue being drawn in with your breath. When you breathe out let go of all judgments and release all negativity and tension. Use the color red and see the cloud exiting your body on your exhale, imagine it disappearing. Now sit in the existence of an open heart and mind and just allow.

Using a small mirror or reflective surface, begin to stare into your face, look with love. Notice the features of your face, your skin, the way your hair outlines your dimensions. Study your eyes, look deep within them. Notice the colors and shapes of any little specs. Looking deep within your eyes, ask yourself, "Why do you dislike me?" "Where did it come from?" Try to think back, "When did it start?"

I'm posing these questions to ponder, but please understand, what I write next is imperative to grasp, these details don't matter! The questions from within each individual are unique, every soul knows what is necessary, so you will know exactly what to ask yourself. Take your time and ask what you will. Posing the questions help open the heart and mind connection between the you looking in the mirror and the you in the mirror. So remind yourself and know the answers aren't important. We dropped the inside information remember? Where, when and even why, makes no difference now.

While intently facing yourself, ask for forgiveness. Seek forgiveness in your eyes, not only for yourself but others. Everyone who has ever upset you, broke your heart, everyone who ever hurt or wronged you in any way. Say "I forgive you." Keep looking in your eyes because you may not see it right away. I wanted to throw my mirror several times and just continue to curse myself, but I refused to give up. I've wasted many years in anger and hatred, so believe me, this was not easy, but 'it's hard' is not an excuse to give up. Undoubtedly, this will bring up many very strong feelings.

One of my first observations was how I was always able to quickly forgive others, why not myself? Don't I deserve as much consideration as anyone else and if I don't think so, why? No matter how you feel about it, apologize to yourself for any wrongdoing. Say I love you and mean I love you! Again, take all the time you need, this may be one of the most important acts of your life. Don't give up—You are worth it!

There is a great quote attributed to Gandhi: "Don't hold a grudge; it allows a person to live in your head rent-free." If there is someone receiving free rent in your head make the effort to forgive and clear the space. Remember, you don't have to call this person, as I feel we are all one and self forgiveness is the key, calling each individual is not necessary. Just reach inside and clear the space, forgive yourself.

The issue with asking another for forgiveness is that we are all on separate spiritual paths and rarely in the same place at the same time. So if you do ask, be aware they may not be ready. That's OK, you will still gain your happiness, time and health back. Our personal healing is most important and the only aspect of forgiveness we can control. Until we help and heal ourselves we cannot begin to help or deal with others.

Looking into your eyes in the mirror ask for forgiveness again, offer to start new from this moment forward. Make a promise that you will show more forgiveness, compassion and gratitude to yourself, as well as others. Your love will know no bounds. Grasping the distinction that details are just part of the story that holds you back can help set you free. The past really doesn't matter in your new outlook.

Eventually, your eyes will soften and see with love again. Forgiveness will come with a flicker of light followed by a flood of passion. You may even see something you've never seen before—*You*. No longer suffocated by a negative story or suffering from needle-like memories you will see a person open to the possibilities of being. A new life begins now that you are free. When you recognize the change, wisdom will come from all sides.

You don't have to run away, you are the pilot, you decide whether you go or stay, paint or play. What you give your time and energy to are crucial decisions to your happiness and are now your choices again. A new path of endless opportunity lay before you.

Once I did this exercise I experienced some immediate positive results and I'm still realizing the long term benefits. Of the many tremendous rewards I noticed was my meditations took on a new high. During a reflective meditation this came to me and I believe it is relative because it emphasizes our relationship with all things.

I Remember!

I remember being energy, fantastic and wild, vibrating through space.

I was all I could be.

Then I remember being a star, bright and shining, lighting up space all around me.

Suddenly, I remember being a plant. How amazing to be utilizing the light that I once gave.

Growing and contributing in so many ways. By breathing I provided oxygen and I expressed joy in brilliant shapes and colors.

Next, I remember being an animal. Truly powerful, I was mobile and could spread love everywhere.

Service to others was my highest calling and I Loved!

Then... I remember nothing, for now being human I find I have forgotten all I once was. The connections once felt now seem faint or missing. Was it all a dream?

All my greatness awaits me re-membering who I AM.

In my silence the link is being retrieved, love coming around again.

I remember being all things and all things remember me.
This is key. I understand what happens to one, happens to all.
*   This is the 'eye of the needle'.*
I am grateful for this inner light, it is the power of love and love
*   is truth.*
Knowing who I AM, I speak, I breathe.

These passionate feelings of connection help explain why I live and die with every plant, animal and life in the world. I am so grateful, I remember we are one. The next new frontier isn't space, it's within our minds and hearts. Making these breakthroughs are imperative to manifesting the type of reality we want moving through this millennium and beyond.

Chapter Four

TRANSFORM YOUR LIFE

There is a tremendous and wonderful energy in the air. Long time, UN-serving habits are coming to an end. Veils are being lifted and truths are coming out. I believe this year to be a time of great transformation. A transformation takes place when you go from being stopped by something to being empowered. It doesn't mean nothing bad will ever happen to you again, but it does mean you will not react in the same old way. To do this you must shift your thought patterns from what you can't do to what you are willing to do. Think in line with your goals.

The time is now! Well done, self forgiveness is the hardest step. However, to stay on this path it takes practice. Successfully forgiving and seeing with new eyes, again, does not mean that you will be ignorant of woe. What it does mean is that you always have your own back. Self forgiveness and awareness open the door to unlimited, rarely tapped potential of being; a well of inner strength, open and available, whenever you need.

There are a few habits and modifications that will help keep you on this journey. A good suggestion is to avoid generalizing. A generalization hides the facts, keeps the hurt persistent and robs our power to deal with the truth. Try to be specific in your speech. Another one is the use of ultimatums, the attitude of 'all or nothing' is also toxic and needs to be eliminated. Be flexible about life, remember, a truly happy person will enjoy the scenery on a detour. In addition, there is the mistake of 'should-ING' on oneself, avoid would'a, could'a, 'should'a, at all cost.

Be happy with what is. With a few minor adjustments you will find, sooner than you might imagine, the feelings of anger that made you react the old way won't be there. Your thoughts will be free to think about the now and plan the future.

Open your heart, feel young again and look at everything with new eyes. The process of forgiveness is not complete until you look at people and events with these new eyes and without any harbored feelings. Have patience and know we all are a work in progress. You'll know your healing when you can think of the people that have done you harm and wish them well. The art of constantly regulating your thoughts will allow your mind to avoid negatives and focus on the positives. Practice being grateful and open to new ideas, then you are well on your way to success.

Declare yourself responsible for your own vibration then live in the possibility of what you want out of life. This is what we are to concentrate on. Here's an example: The other day I had a situation that caused me great stress and I felt my husband didn't understand. The old me would have not only argued but yelled. The new me just sat down and thought about it instead. The best first reaction is NO reaction at all.

A great practice before you act or even think is to *breathe*. I did not verbalize my negative thoughts or complain for my feelings, rather, I replayed the situation as a fly on the wall. In a few moments, without me fueling the fire with existing story-lines, my anger petered out and I was glad I hadn't said anything that I would most likely later regret. I was quickly able to see it was no big deal and move on, still aligned with my goals. This is very important because we may not be able to control what happens to us, but we certainly can control how we react.

The best we can do is be happy in our own space and act consistent with who we are. Go beyond forgiveness into a whole different mode of thinking. When we go from thoughts of revenge to wishing people love we are walking our spiritual path. This is what I call being responsible for our own energy, our own vibration.

We have a new power now and we act on our potential, not our feelings. This extends to all aspects of life and all creatures. For instance, if I see a spider on the wall, I no longer get caught up in details of whether or not I like spiders, whether I've been bitten by a spider or if they invoke fear. Living in the now, my only concern is if the spider is in a good place for it's well-being. I carefully remove them from inside the premises. Everything I do now, I do with love.

Try to look at everything through loving eyes, attempt to put yourself in the others position, or at least be an unbiased bystander aka 'fly on the wall'. This may or may not be noticed by other people and that doesn't matter because you will notice your happiness greatly increase and things just won't have the power over you they once did.

Not living in the UN-serving details of our story is a huge step. Within days of my self-forgiveness I started noticing things I would not have thought related if it weren't for the incredible mounting evidence. Little things, at first, like feeling more refreshed on less sleep, being more organized without trying. An undeniable flow and a overwhelming joy.

There are still stresses hitting me, yes, but I'm responding to them in a whole new way. I've noticed less distraction in my studies and I'm getting a lot more done in less time. In an age when time seems to be the greatest commodity, efficiency makes a world of difference. As I said before, doing this work not only increases happiness it increases energy, clarity and even humor in life. Now that I've gained control of my thoughts and I practice focusing on positives I find everything so entertaining. It's brilliantly true, laughter is good for the soul and we are in a divine comedy.

Three of the major benefits I've noticed since my forgiveness are faster healing times, much better response to conflict and improved organization. First, my cat badly scratched my hand and in the past I would have had that scratch six months. I've been slow to heal for years however, this cut and all evidence of it was gone in three days! I could hardly believe it.

This made me wonder how much of what we feel about ourselves has to do with our health and our ability to heal? From six months to three days because of forgiveness—Amazing!

Second, the comfort of feeling 'whole' again has far-reaching benefits. The other day I received some bad news and was a little down. Immediately, I felt arms around me and a great comfort coming from within. I feel good with myself, without need of anyone or anything else.

We're always looking for, in other people or items, what we can only really find in ourselves. I hear some say 'if he/she would only love me more, I would feel better.' The truth is much simpler. If we would only love ourselves more we would feel the reinforcement that we need and wouldn't long for outside love, but instead gratefully accept it for the precious gift that it is. I'm completely fascinated by my new found abilities. No matter what happens I have strength to combat negative thinking with new posture and the skills to turn it into positive fuel.

In every breakdown be grateful that the experience you think is a set back actually catapults you to the breakthrough you need for life. With the help of your new insights, motivation, goals and clear perception you are compelled to excel at will. You are truly able to accept and share love in a new way, increase the amount of laughter and joy in your life and find humor in just about everything.

It is amazing how impossible it is to be upset when you're laughing. Try it. Even if it starts with a little effort it quickly grows to genuine fun and immediately raises our vibrations. I suspect the 'laughing Buddha' knew this. By diligently using these new skills I no longer find myself replaying the past or stressing about the future, I am right where I should be. Happily experiencing the now.

The third ongoing benefit I am noticing is a 'no effort', new me. For the last few years I have struggled to be organized, always rushing at the last minute, losing my keys or worse, my wallet. Now I'm flowing with everything so effortlessly.

I have not lost my keys, wallet or anything else. In fact, I'm always well-packed and ahead of schedule. I don't even use an alarm clock anymore. I feel in accord with myself, my house, my environment, relationships and nature. I'm so happy and I have so much more time. My studies have tripled and my health skyrocketed.

Other supportive behavior that I practice and highly recommend is aromatherapy, beating drums and dancing, eating healthy, drinking a detox juice once a month and exercising two to three days a week. None of these come with undue effort, it's what I enjoy doing in my new balanced life. In fact, all of these changes have come quite naturally as I now have a clear commitment to myself.

I struggled with meditation in the past but not anymore and I highly recommend this custom as well. Meditation and silence opens the opportunity to go within and allows us to connect with our higher being. In doing so we find inner peace. The practice of meditation greatly improves one's life. As Rumi said "I'm looking for the secrets to the mysteries of the world, someone said to me. . Shhh . . . Silence will tell you about the secrets to the mysteries of the world."

With all the positive changes I was feeling like a whirlwind so I had to ask myself 'what's going on'? The answer came back abundantly clear—forgiveness heals! We have the power to heal our body and mind. The practice of being grateful for what we have attracts more of what we want. Through this, our spirit soars.

Forgiveness puts us back in accord with Source and brings harmony to our lives. Now I look to act in the possibility of freedom, in a way that empowers me. I am grateful for the opportunities life gives me to grow, learn and love. Through good times and hard, the universe and I have my back!

I'm grateful for the people who act out what the universe is teaching me, for I know without them, I couldn't learn as fast or as much. If there were no challenges how could I grow? So I am even grateful for those who shake my very core, forcing me to think, allowing me the opportunity to practice my patience, faith, strength and resolve. Thank you and much love to all. This is the art of love.

In my new life it's time to take my message to the world. With the winds of change sweeping the Earth, transformation is happening on a global level. However, when it comes to power to change the world I still know there is more we can do. Meditation and coherency of the heart is the tremendous, untapped potential. We can change all minds and hearts with our minds and hearts.

I read a quote by Mother Teresa, 'An anti-war rally, this I would never attend but have a peace rally and I'll be there.' This is so profound because what we resist, persists. There's more we can do than just resisting so let's exercise our real strength.

I also believe as Albert Einstein did that 'no problem can be solved in the same consciousness that created it.' We must forgive. To truly bring about lasting change, a real paradigm shift, we must do what has never been done before—go within. It has to start somewhere. It has to start with me, it has to start with you, it has to start now from within.

Later in Chapter 5 we look at the work being done in understanding consciousness, intentions and random number generators, proving that the power of intention and the global consciousness is real. If ten or twenty thousand people dropped their hatred, our interpersonal dynamic would change overnight!

The inner power is the true power. Even the strongest of people can be physically overcome or repressed but none who tap into their inner power can be shaken, controlled, mentally imprisoned or even told a lie. Our heart knows, when the heart is open all is revealed. No one can manipulate you and nothing can be hidden. So long as we look within.

Looking with love is the power they continually distract us from seeing. Food additives, poisons in our air, food and water, anti-depressants being handed out like candy, all ensure our pineal gland is well crusted over and our ability to sit still and look within is greatly impeded. Don't let obstacles like these keep you from realizing your true power. Power that makes every protest, through all of history combined, look like child's play. Forgive yourself and forgive others. From this space realize there are No barriers, No separations, No problems and No fear.

We can change the world NOW without lifting one finger, standing in one line or meeting one politician. We can change their minds and hearts with our minds and hearts. The same qualities that Jesus, Mother Teresa, Gandhi and others have used to bring about real change. More people are discovering these truths and are now living rewarding lives free from disease, fear and anger.

Consider the words of Stuart Wilde "The spiritual journey through life is only four feet long, travel one foot down from your head to your Heart and three feet outward to embrace the first human you meet."

Grace carries it's own strength and it's vibration can be felt all over the world. People change in it's presence without even knowing how or why. We don't need just a regime change, we need a thoughts-shift out of the body and into the heart! Everything happens for a purpose. We may not see the wisdom of it all now but believe that everything is for the best and we are shown these lessons for reason. I like to say whatever doesn't kill us will continue to wake us up. There is a tremendous amount of freedom in this acceptance.

Choose to be at peace. In this mindset human beings are capable of miraculous changes. I believe C. Wright Mills statement, "In our time, what is at issue is the very nature of humankind, the image we have of our limits and possibilities. History is not yet done with its exploration of the limits of what it means to be human."

An interesting note that fascinates me is that those who activate their Mer Ka Ba, which is our light-spirit-body field, are said to look like stars on the planet from space. I think this is very appropriate given we are made of star dust with star energy. Coincidence?

Chapter Five

PROOF IN SCIENCE

Being so powerfully moved by my experiences of quick healing and transformation, I researched confirmation in support of my theories. I found there to be a mounting body of scientific evidence behind the idea that forgiveness heals and thoughts rule our life. There are many verifiable phenomenon surrounding these concepts. With so much supporting documentation, I invite you to do your own research, however I do want to highlight a few of these miraculous findings.

Look at the 'Copenhagen Thesis' in quantum mechanics. It is agreed, there is no objective reality. Which means everything comes from within. Other studies show that we can change the way reality behaves just by looking at it. The popularized version of this is the 'double-slit experiment' in quantum mechanics.

The double-slit experiment shows that matter and energy can display characteristics of both waves and particles. This demonstrates a powerful realization that the observer affects the outcome. Our intentions, thoughts and feelings continually create our reality. Remember, there is no such thing as 'out there' everything exists within.

The Institute of Noetic Sciences was founded by Astronaut and visionary Edgar D. Mitchell ScD, PhD. The institute is showing amazing research in the fields of mind/body connections. Mr. Mitchell said "There are no unnatural or supernatural phenomena, only very large gaps in our knowledge of what is natural, particularly regarding relatively rare occurrences."

The lead scientist at IONS is Dean Radin PhD. and he is on the leading edge of consciousness studies, proving astonishing connections between thought and physical manifestation. One of the first studies to capture the public is the work done on 'random number generators'. In a terrific interview on the IONS website: "Intention Downloads Interview: Dr. Edgar Mitchell states 'Dean Radin there at Noetics, has done work in demonstrating that both intention and attention create changes in random number generators, and very similar work in seeing the effect of mind state on random number generators.'

Among the many books Dr. Radin has written, one of my favorites that also explains this connection is "The Conscious Universe: The Scientific Proof of Psychic Phenomena" (HarperOne 2009) deanradin.com.

More incredible information can be found at the HeartMath Institute. The Institute of Heartmath has proven "The heart is the most powerful generator of rhythmic information patterns in the human body." So doesn't it stand to reason that if the heart is troubled so shall the body suffer? HeartMath has proven, in a number of studies, that people who forgive are happier and healthier than those who hold resentments.

Forgiveness results in "states of psycho-physiological coherence". Our inner systems function with a higher degree of synchronization, efficiency and harmony thereby increasing emotional well-being and cognitive performance. It's amazing work, they discover something new everyday and are quickly helping to fill the vast gaps in our knowledge about ourselves and our world.

The University of Wisconsin-Madison is exploring the questions of how forgiveness improves physical health. Led by Robert D. Enright, Professor of educational psychology. They discovered that people only need to think about forgiving to improve functioning in their cardiovascular and nervous systems. Research showed the more forgiving people were, the less they suffered from a wide range of illnesses, while the less forgiving people reported a greater number of health problems.

Fred Luskin PhD. Of Stanford University is the Director of the Stanford University Forgiveness Projects and an Associate Professor at the Institute of Transpersonal Psychology. His studies found that people who are taught how to forgive don't get as angry or hurt and are overall more optimistic. The people exposed to the practice are also more forgiving, compassionate and self-confident. Those with the ability to forgive show a reduction in stress and illness, while showing an increase in vitality. (Conversations with Fred Luskin, PhD 2003) This is tremendous evidence for the art of forgiving. To think this all is this comes from within.

Kinetic Forgiveness is an interesting concept that places an emphasis on removing the negative patterns, thoughts and emotions that remain in the memory as an unhealthy attachment to the past trauma. This is also known as the mind/body connection.

Betty J. Humphrey wrote in her book entitled "Kinetic Forgiveness: Learning to Forgive Like God" Published by CreateSpace (October 13, 2011) 'So long as there is a negative reaction that can be triggered by remembering a person or event, those reactions in themselves will block healing for that individual.' Information regarding this has been found as far back as Sanskrit tablets, information explaining the power of the mind/body and heart/mind connections which play key roles in our ability to break through normal realms into higher vibrations and energy resources.

Research by <u>Rev. Michael Barry, Author of "The Forgiveness Project"</u> seems to clearly illustrate the relationship between forgiveness and the immune system. Rev. Barry describes unforgiving to be "a form of cancer that can spread into every area of our lives", his studies have shown there to be an "increase in health when forgiveness is practiced by those facing a long term illness." It's also shown to be a very effective tool for letting go of negativity and anger.

He is part of a grand effort to help distribute this information and set the world free. Progress like this makes me very excited for our future. For more information read "The Forgiveness Project: The Startling Discovery of How to Overcome Cancer, Find Health, and Achieve Peace" Published by Kregel Publications (January 2011).

One of my favorite ideas of forgiveness comes from a Hawaiian tradition called Ho'oponopono (ho-o-pono-pono). This is an ancient Hawaiian practice of reconciliation and forgiveness. Ho means 'to', Ponopono is to 'correct'. Their saying goes 'If you are angry for two or three days, sickness will come.

They know we must keep our energy field clear. The technique to achieve this is Ho'oponopono. It is an ancient code of forgiveness, used to correct the things that have gone wrong in a person's life. This Hawaiian tradition emphasizes prayer, confession, repentance and mutual forgiveness. To empty ourselves of negative experiences clears the path for healing.

According to the ancient Hawaiians, error arises from thoughts that are tainted by painful memories but Ho'oponopono offers a way to release the energy of these painful 'errors' which cause imbalance and dis-ease. I like this and believe we must stand in our TRUTH for balance and harmony.

Last but most inspirational to me, all the work from <u>Louise L Hay.</u> Inspirational author and Publisher. She is the founder of Hay House Publishing and the Hay Foundation. Louise has assisted with many truly amazing transformations. Regarded as one of the founders of the mirror exercise Louise Hay has done extensive reflective work over the years and I highly recommend "You Can Heal Your Life" (1984) and "The Power is Within You" (1991). Two of my favorites are "You Can Heal Your Life" and "Receiving Prosperity" (1991). Her first book "Heal Your Body" (1976) was before it's time in discussing our mind-body connection.

Chapter Six

A WORD ABOUT VIBRATION

A little note about vibration. Many aren't yet aware or are struggling with the idea of the Unseen World. Vibration—What is it and how do we know when ours has been affected? We have been raised and bombarded with the notion that nothing exists outside our five senses. If we can't taste, smell, see, touch or hear something it cannot, must not exist.

In the past if we thought otherwise we might be put under peer pressure and even professional scrutiny as being 'nuts'. We police each other effectively, but unfortunately, not for the betterment of humanity. Many don't understand why suddenly they may feel sick or confused when they see or hear something. They describe it as literally being hit with a negative wave. This is our inner voice telling us something is not right, not truth, maybe even not human. Our vibration has been altered.

Many things we can't see or don't understand slows our vibrational energy. Some we have control over like our thoughts, language, food and drink. Some we don't.

Take sarcasm, as one example, one of my least favorite responses to an uncomfortable situation. Most sarcastic remarks are at someone's expense so they have a slight negative hint. Whether the comment is funny or not doesn't seem to matter, it will almost always adversely affect the energy of all involved.

The emotions of slow vibrations are at the root of all suffering. This is where we find fear, anger, mistrust, self pity, self loathing, ego, duality, competition, sickness, longing and loss. Interestingly, many things we ingest have the same effect; such as pop, candy, food dyes, genetically modified foods and especially additives like aspartame, high fructose corn syrup and sugar. These foods should be avoided.

It's not just food, try and also resist people's bad attitudes, stay away from unhappy complainers who refuse to change and particularly avoid T.V. The television is filled with propaganda always pushing you to buy more, compare your life with others, keep up with the Jones' and soap opera's telling you this is the way of life. Instead, delight in what you want to see and hear. Make responsible choices to further your spiritual growth and protect your vibration.

If you feel sick or burst out in laughter at a seemingly inappropriate time it might be your BS bell going off. Something is talking to you. Don't just ignore these feelings, get angry or medicate, explore them and investigate who or what it is around you making you feel that way and avoid them or that.

We must each take responsibility for our own vibration. We may do what makes us feel good as long as it hurts no being in the universe and is aligned with truth. Deflect that which brings you down, listen to your inner voice and take control. Your heart and gut feelings will never steer you wrong.

Living in the harmony of the heart and mind, we're open to truth and have no need to fear. Some good ways to raise vibration is to do the things we love, I like to take a walk in nature, dance, sing, be with family and friends. Eat foods with Light in them, that is to say, fresh foods, raw preferably, not frozen, canned, processed or microwaved. Spend time with animals, for they have an inner sense of harmony as well and this tends to meld with us as we enter into a state of coherence with them. To love the things you do, do the things you love.

It sounds a little Hollywood but the ideas in movies like 'Star Wars' (George Lucas, 1977) were not complete fantasy. There is a "force" all around us and inside of us. In fact, I believe many sayings we know well prove this but we don't realize it because their origins have been lost. For example, the 'truth resonates within' which means does it fit your vibration? Does it sit well with you? Take what does and leave the rest.

Another one is 'God helps those that help themselves' which means make the effort and the universe will support you. This also means avoiding the things we know are not good for us. This goes with 'ignorance is not an excuse' because we do know better when we look in our hearts. All the correct answers are within. The tiny, sometimes inaudible voice deep down inside truly knows. That's the voice we need to rejoice with, that's the existence we need to remember, our intimate connection with Source.

Every single true prophet and teacher in history have actually given the exact same message, we have only been mislead to believe they are in conflict. It makes sense that each land and people of the earth would need someone they could relate to and trust to speak the universal truth, so there had to be many.

Soon it will come clear as the time for separation comes to an end, that we are all one and they really did have the same message; Love. Our level of vibration is very important and we all need to take responsibility for what we bring to this reality.

Quite often, we find ourselves conforming to a frequency that isn't ours. This creates a great amount of discomfort. By proclaiming our truth with love, we start processes that protect us from lower vibrational hits and may even positively influence others. When this happens on a global scale, unity will immediately be present. Knowing there is a better way I choose not to take part in campaigns of fear, grudges or resentments.

We have been taught fear, but that is over now. Fear is not a viable way of living. Only love can deliver us. Thank you for helping to heal the planet by healing yourself and loving others. By actively working on forgiveness, kindness and compassion we will all live in a better place.

Most people are really wonderful, honest, deserving people, who just need a little respect and love. Some need a helping hand, but all of which we come to know, not as strangers but as aspects of ourselves.

This is where NDE's (near death experiences) come in handy. They allow us to realize very quickly that we are not separate. They allow us to experience the realms others only guess about and for this I am grateful.

I am the first survivor of Niceria Meningococcal meningitis, in history. It is a very wicked, rare disease that had a three day incubation/death period before me. I had it over a week in 1993 before I finally died upon arrival to the ER. I'm grateful to say, because of antibodies in my blood, there is now over an 85% survival rate. This was an incredible experience!

After seeing my body on the table and the Doctors pulling out all the stops to save me, I was flowing through a tunnel. I was happy to be in and of the great Light energy. I had no fear, I felt peace and love like never before. Having called it the pure, unconditional love-light and amazing bliss, I realize we just don't have the words in our language to lend the experience justice, but it was brilliant.

I found myself at the base of a mountain. Bathing in an intense but soft forgiving love. A message radiated from my heart and what I was told was not only amazing and profound, it was so simple. You've heard the saying "simplicity is the hallmark of genius", well it's true, in triplicate.

The exact words aren't important but know that our love is the answer, our love is the key, our love is the reservoir of strength we need to make it through this plane of existence. Not only is love the destination but it is the vehicle and the road too!

There is a saying by the Buddha "When you realize how simple it all is you will throw your head back and laugh." This is truth! My mind was so moved by how easy it is, I broke out laughing almost hysterically. I begged to return so I could share it with the world. Though I really didn't want to leave the unconditional love-light, I felt I must to try and help others understand, it is so simple. Love one another and ourselves. Love ourselves to love one another. It's not difficult and the benefits are astounding.

I think everyone should have an NDE every 3-5 years to get and keep a proper perspective on the truth of what is important. We tend to lose these concepts over time as our thoughts get convoluted with everyday life. We must not allow ourselves to live as though asleep. We are extraordinary beings with immense power and this is a great responsibility.

Chapter Seven

BEST WISHES

Make all the years the best years of your life, with love, forgiveness and compassion for all! You have my love and support. I believe the tipping point has been reached. Our collective compassion has moved beyond our need for toys and Mankind is evolving into Kind-Man. Thank you for standing up and being part of the wave of healing. I'm so grateful, it would take me a lifetime to count my blessings, but I am going to count them, I am going to count them all.

Namaste means 'I bow to you', it is the most loving, respectful salutation I can offer and it is yours. I like to say my inner Light recognizes your inner Light for they are the same Light. I hope you have enjoyed this book and use the exercises to let go of uncomfortable feelings and negative thoughts that obstruct happiness and cause illness. Now embrace the free and powerful life you want by controlling your thoughts and emotions for a better life.

Please Review this book. As well, I would love to hear from you. Questions and comments are always welcome.

PleaseContact:

JudeneElizabeth@gmail.com

BONUS MATERIAL

One of the reasons I love meditation so much is it allows access to experiences the otherwise unknown. These lucid moments teach us about ourselves. Recently while enjoying a particularly powerful meditation, this came to me with all the vision and sound of a most fantastic voyage. Not even Hollywood can produce such amazing sights . .

I went out into the formlessness so vast and flowing
I heard voices saying 'I'm not going to let go' and I brushed them
*   away with a wave of my hand.*
Out further into the void I went, enjoying the energy of
*   everything.*
I saw dolphins 'swimming' in the sea of formlessness,
So inviting and free.
So incredible to feel what it is to be me.
Without thought, listening to the silence
Aware of the stillness, becoming the vastness
Perfectly calm, yet yearning to use words which cannot display
*   my being.*

*The dangling patterns in the air look complicated but seem ever
flowing free of such trivial substance.*

*My love is an invisible touch into the universe like rippling
waves, sharing, caring and vibrating the all.*

*Witnessing the oscillations of vast brilliance I realize now it is
the ocean of consciousness.*

*Watching dolphins in blissful dances going around and through
the shapes in space*

So beautiful, perfect and free, open somehow anticipating—me.

*I am all that is, known to be the energy of this canvas I go from
observer to creator and my heart's desire fills the void*

*Spewing colors and shapes presented before me more acute
than my two eyes have ever seen, I float with fascination
and admiration for all I wonder*

Somehow I'm home in the comfort that we are one,

The ocean is me!

*I feel the advancement of the cosmic soul like a heartbeat in
the wind.*

Sharing great love...

Back into the stillness I go

AUTHOR BIOGRAPHY

Judene Elizabeth is a bright and busy young writer. She has been writing for many years but has only recently understood enough self worth, confidence and forgiveness to undergo the publishing process. Thereby, proving this method really works.

She has many projects in the works ranging from a science fiction trilogy to a complete DIY Off grid project series. Her next book is about holding White Light Vibrations among chaotic circumstances, look for it soon.

Printed in the United States
By Bookmasters